AF492560

Be Basic

Spice Cabinet Staples

No Frills Cookbook Collection
Volume One

Emmy Gatrell

Relevant Daearen

Dedicated to everyone that clicks...

'Go to recipe'

Table of Contents

Basics, Directions & Tips

The Basics:

These are all seasoning mixes. They mostly use dry ingredients that require just a sift or a minimal amount of work.

Spice mixes lose their flavor over time, usually 3-6 months on a cool dark shelf. I live in a moisture-rich environment, so I keep most of my mixes in the fridge, especially if they have salt in them, and they last anywhere from 3-12 months.

Instructions:

Unless specifically noted, add all ingredients in a bowl and sift them together.

You can use it right away or funnel into an airtight jar or bottle for later.

OR Skip the bowl, put spices directly into the jar, close tightly, and shake to mix.

Tips & Notes:

Clean & reuse your old spice bottles. The shaker tops come in handy!

Seasoning mixes make fantastic gifts! Leave the spices layered (They are so pretty this way! It looks like bottle sand art!) or premix spices in a huge batch, then fill in jars. Add a cute label, and you're done!

Author's Notes Before You Begin

Measuring:

I use American Standard Measurements / Imperial Measuring System in my recipes, but if you live anywhere else in the world, you probably go by weight and volume. Please refer to the chart at the back of the book to convert your measurements.

Salt:

I use coarse salt in almost all my recipes, if you don't have coarse salt, please refer to the chart at the back of the book to substitute the kind of salt you have available.

Dried vs. Fresh Ingredients:

If you want to be adventurous and mix up a batch using fresh ingredients, follow the conversion charts at the back of the book to figure out the correct amounts.

Dry mixes, you'll want to use them toward the end of your cook time.

Mixes using fresh ingredients, you'll want to use at the beginning of your cook time.

Spice Cabinet Staples

Allspice (Copycat)

Yield: A little less than ¼ cup

1 tablespoon **GROUND CINNAMON**

1 tablespoon **GROUND CLOVES**

1 tablespoon **GROUND NUTMEG**

Celery Salt

Yield: About ½ cup

¼ cup **CELERY SEEDS**

½ cup **COARSE SEA SALT**

Instructions:

1. Put celery seeds and salt in a grinder and grind to desired consistency.

Chili Powder

Yield: About ½ cup

¼ cup **PAPRIKA**

1 ½ tablespoon **DRIED OREGANO**

1 tablespoon **GROUND CUMIN**

1 tablespoon **GARLIC POWDER**

½ tablespoon **ONION POWDER**

½ - 1 teaspoon **GROUND CAYENNE PEPPER**

Chili Powder (Smoky)

Yield: About ½ cup

¼ cup **SMOKED PAPRIKA**

1 ½ tablespoon **DRIED OREGANO**

1 tablespoon **GROUND CUMIN**

1 tablespoon **GARLIC POWDER**

½ tablespoon **ONION POWDER**

½ - 1 teaspoon **GROUND CAYENNE PEPPER**

Chili Powder (Smoky & Spicy)

Yield: About ⅔ cup

¼ cup **SMOKED PAPRIKA**

1 ½ tablespoon **DRIED OREGANO**

1 tablespoon **GROUND CUMIN**

1 tablespoon **GARLIC POWDER**

1 tablespoon **GROUND CAYENNE PEPPER**

1 tablespoon **DRIED RED CHILE PEPPER FLAKES**

½ tablespoon **ONION POWDER**

Chili Powder (Spicy)

Yield: About ⅔ cup

¼ cup **PAPRIKA**

1 ½ tablespoon **DRIED OREGANO**

1 tablespoon **GROUND CUMIN**

1 tablespoon **GARLIC POWDER**

1 tablespoon **GROUND CAYENNE PEPPER**

1 tablespoon **DRIED RED CHILE PEPPER FLAKES**

½ tablespoon **ONION POWDER**

Lemon Pepper

Yield: About ½ cup

½ cup **BLACK PEPPERCORNS**

2 ½ tablespoons **DRIED LEMON PEEL**

Instructions:

1. Combine ingredients in a grinder or food processor and pulse until everything is coarsely ground.

Lemon Pepper Seasoning

Yield: About 1 cup

½ cup **BLACK PEPPERCORNS**

2 ½ tablespoons **DRIED LEMON PEEL**

2 tablespoons **DRIED CHOPPED ONION**

2 tablespoons **DRIED THYME**

1 ½ tablespoons **CORIANDER SEEDS**

Instructions:

1. Combine all ingredients in a grinder or food processor and pulse until everything is coarsely ground.

My House Seasoning

Yield: About ¼ cup

½ tablespoon **BLACK PEPPERCORNS**

½ tablespoon **CORIANDER SEEDS**

½ tablespoon **DRIED THYME**

½ tablespoon **DRIED OREGANO**

½ tablespoon **DRIED BASIL**

½ tablespoon **DRIED PARSLEY**

½ tablespoon **DRIED ROSEMARY**

½ tablespoon **MUSTARD POWDER**

½ tablespoon **ONION POWDER**

½ tablespoon **GARLIC POWDER**

Instructions:

1. Put peppercorns and coriander in food processor and pulse until coarsely ground.
2. Add everything else to the processor and pulse a couple of times until well blended.

*I tend to use the same spices in many dishes, so I made a mix to save time. If you don't use some of these or use other ingredients, switch whatever you want out or add whatever you want to 'your house seasoning.'

Your House Seasoning

Figure out what spices you're always reaching for in the kitchen. Start with equal amounts of each. Taste and adjust to your family's liking.

No-Salt Seasoning 'Salt'

Yield: About ⅓ cup

2 tablespoons **ONION POWDER**

1 tablespoon **PAPRIKA**

1 tablespoon **GARLIC POWDER**

1 tablespoon **GROUND MUSTARD**

1 teaspoon **DRIED THYME**

½ teaspoon **DRIED BASIL**

½ teaspoon **GROUND BLACK PEPPER**

***** Add in place of salt in recipes **BUT NOT** in baked goods!

<u>**Spicy Seasoning Salt**</u>

Yield: Just under ½ cup

1 tablespoon **FINE SALT**

1 tablespoon **GROUND BLACK PEPPER**

1 tablespoon **ONION POWDER**

1 tablespoon **GARLIC POWDER**

½ tablespoon **CHILI POWDER**

½ tablespoon **PAPRIKA**

½ tablespoon **DRIED PARSLEY**

½ tablespoon **DRIED RED CHILE PEPPER FLAKES**

½ tablespoon **GROUND CAYENNE PEPPER**

½ tablespoon **GROUND CUMIN**

Taco Seasoning

Yield: About 2 cups

½ cup **FLOUR**

¼ cup **CHILI POWDER**

¼ cup **GROUND CUMIN**

¼ cup **GROUND CORIANDER**

¼ cup **DRIED CILANTRO**

2 tablespoons **GARLIC POWDER**

2 tablespoons **ONION POWDER**

1 tablespoon **DRIED OREGANO**

1 tablespoon **PAPRIKA**

1 tablespoon **COARSE SEA SALT** (optional)

1½ teaspoons **GROUND BLACK PEPPER** (reduce for less heat)

1 teaspoon **DRIED RED CHILE PEPPER FLAKES** (optional)

*¼ cup = 1 store-bought packet

Taco Meat Recipe

1. One pound ground meat of choice browned, drained, put back in the pan.
2. Add ⅔ cup water & ¼ cup seasoning; cook, often stirring, until thickened.

Taco Dip Recipe

1. 16 ounces softened cream cheese (full, light, or fat-free) and add Taco seasoning mix to taste. (Start with ¼ cup, then keep adding, mixing, and tasting until you like it.)
2. Spread on cookie sheet top with cheese, lettuce, tomatoes, onions, etc.

Sweets
&
Baking

Apple Pie Spice

Yield: About ½ cup

6 tablespoons **GROUND CINNAMON**

2 teaspoons **GROUND NUTMEG**

2 teaspoons **GROUND CARDAMOM**

1 teaspoon **GROUND GINGER**

½ teaspoons **GROUND ALLSPICE**

Cardamom Sugar

Yield: About ¼ cup

10 **CARDAMOM PODS**, (or more to taste)

¼ cup **WHITE SUGAR**

Instructions:

1. Crack cardamom pods open to remove seeds. Discard husks.
2. Combine cardamom seeds and 2 tablespoons sugar in a spice grinder; grind until fine. Combine with remaining sugar.

Chai

Yield: About ¼ cup

1 ½ tablespoons **GROUND GINGER**

1 tablespoon **GROUND CINNAMON**

2 teaspoons **GROUND CARDAMOM**

1 ½ teaspoons **GROUND ALLSPICE**

1 ½ teaspoons **GROUND CLOVES**

Cinnamon Sugar

Yield: About ⅔ cup

½ cup **GRANULATED SUGAR**

1-2 tablespoons **GROUND CINNAMON**

Spicy Cinnamon-Sugar

Yield: About ⅔ cup

½ cup **GRANULATED SUGAR**

1-2 tablespoons **GROUND CINNAMON**

¼ - ½ teaspoon **GROUND CAYENNE PEPPER**

Gingerbread Spice

Yield: About ¼ cup

1 tablespoon **GROUND CINNAMON**

1 tablespoon **GROUND GINGER**

1 tablespoon **GROUND ALLSPICE**

½ tablespoons **GROUND NUTMEG**

½ tablespoons **GROUND CLOVES**

dash **GROUND BLACK PEPPER**

*Gingerbread spice can be used in place of cinnamon in many recipes.

Pumpkin Pie Spice

Yield: About ⅓ cup

¼ cup **GROUND CINNAMON**

2 teaspoons **GROUND NUTMEG**

2 teaspoons **GROUND ALLSPICE**

1 teaspoon **GROUND GINGER**

½ teaspoons **GROUND CLOVES** (optional)

<u>**Vanilla Sugar**</u>

1-2 **WHOLE VANILLA BEANS**

SUGAR

<u>Instructions:</u>

1. Put 1-2 good quality whole vanilla beans in a jar or reuse a clean old spice bottle, then fill it with sugar (white, natural, raw, they all work) and shake, wait a week, and it's good to go.
2. When the sugar gets low, just add more sugar to the jar and shake it!

*Some folks say the vanilla beans last only a year… but I've used the same beans in my vanilla sugar for much longer.

Special Seasoning Mixes

Buffalo Seasoning

Yield: About ⅓ cup

2 tablespoons **BROWN SUGAR**

1 tablespoon **GARLIC POWDER**

2 teaspoons **GROUND CAYENNE CHILE PEPPER**

2 teaspoons **GROUND CUMIN**

1 teaspoon **GROUND BLACK PEPPER**

1 teaspoon **SMOKED PAPRIKA**

Cajun Seasoning

Yield: About ⅔ cup

¼ cup **PAPRIKA**

2 ½ tablespoons **COARSE SEA SALT**

2 tablespoons **GARLIC POWDER**

1 tablespoon **ONION POWDER**

1 tablespoon **DRIED OREGANO**

1 tablespoon **DRIED THYME**

½-1 tablespoon **GROUND BLACK PEPPER**

½ tablespoon **GROUND CAYENNE PEPPER** (optional)

Chinese Five-Spice

Yield: A little less than ½ cup

2 tablespoons **GROUND ANISE**

1 tablespoon **GROUND BLACK PEPPER**

1 tablespoon **GROUND FENNEL**

1 tablespoon **GROUND CINNAMON**

1 tablespoon **GROUND CLOVES**

Curry Seasoning

Yield: A little less than ½ cup

2 tablespoons **GROUND CUMIN**

2 tablespoons **GROUND CORIANDER**

2 tablespoons **GROUND TURMERIC**

1 ½ teaspoons **GROUND CARDAMOM**

Everything Bagel Seasoning

Yield: About ¾ cup

3 tablespoons **COARSE SEA SALT**

3 tablespoons **POPPY SEEDS**

3 tablespoons **SESAME SEEDS**

2 tablespoons. **DRIED MINCED GARLIC**

2 tablespoons. **DRIED MINCED ONION**

Instructions:

1. In a small skillet over medium heat, add poppy seeds, sesame seeds, garlic, and onion and cook, continually stirring, until fragrant and lightly browned, about 2 minutes.
2. Transfer to a bowl and stir in salt. Let cool completely. Spice mix can be stored at room temperature in an airtight container for up to 1 month.

Everything Bagel Seasoning (Spicy)

Yield: About ¼ cup

1 ½ tablespoons **SESAME SEEDS**

1 tablespoon **POPPY SEEDS**

1 ½ tablespoons **DRIED CHOPPED ONION**

1 teaspoon **GARLIC POWDER**

Pinch of **FINE SALT**

Large pinch of **DRIED RED CHILE PEPPER FLAKES**

Instructions:

1. In a small skillet over medium heat, add poppy seeds, sesame seeds, garlic, and onion and cook, continually stirring, until fragrant and lightly browned, about 2 minutes.
2. Transfer to a bowl and stir in salt. Let cool completely. Spice mix can be stored at room temperature in an airtight container for up to 1 month.

French Fry Seasoning

Yield: About ⅔ cup

¼ cup **COARSE SEA SALT**

2 tablespoons **PAPRIKA**

1 tablespoon **GARLIC POWDER**

1 tablespoon **GARLIC SALT**

½ tablespoon **GROUND CUMIN**

½ tablespoon **GROUND BLACK PEPPER**

½ tablespoon **DRIED BASIL**

½ tablespoon **DRIED PARSLEY**

1 teaspoon **CHILI POWDER**

½ teaspoon **CELERY SALT**

Garlic Bread Seasoning

Yield: About ¾ cup

½ cup **POWDERED PARMESAN CHEESE**

2 tablespoons **GARLIC POWDER**

2 teaspoons **COARSE SEA SALT**

2 teaspoons **DRIED OREGANO**

2 teaspoons **DRIED BASIL**

2 teaspoons **DRIED MARJORAM**

2 teaspoons **DRIED PARSLEY**

Garlic Bread Recipe

1. Preheat oven to 375°F
2. Combine ¼ cup seasoning with ½ cup (1 stick) of softened butter.
3. Spread garlic butter on a loaf of French bread (cut in ½ lengthwise).
4. Wrap in foil and bake until butter's melted.
5. If you want, you can also put it open-faced under the broiler for a minute or two, so it gets a little crispy.

<u>Gyro Seasoning</u>

Yield: About 1 cup

1 tablespoon **PAPRIKA**

1 tablespoon **GARLIC POWDER**

1 tablespoon **ONION POWDER**

1 tablespoon **GROUND CUMIN**

1 tablespoon **GROUND CORIANDER**

1 tablespoon **DRIED ROSEMARY**, crushed

1 tablespoon **DRIED OREGANO**

1 teaspoon **GROUND CINNAMON**

Hamburger Seasoning

Yield: About ⅔ cup

4 tablespoons **GROUND BLACK PEPPER**

2 tablespoons **PAPRIKA**

2 tablespoons **SMOKED PAPRIKA**

2 teaspoons **FINE SALT**

½ tablespoon **BROWN SUGAR**

½ tablespoon **GARLIC POWDER**

½ tablespoon **ONION POWDER**

1 teaspoon **GROUND CUMIN**

To use: Add 2 teaspoons seasoning for every pound of beef.

Herb and Garlic Seasoning Mix

Yield: Between ¾ - 1 cup

¼ cup **GARLIC POWDER**

¼ cup **ONION POWDER**

¼ cup **DRIED PARSLEY**

1 tablespoon **COARSE SEA SALT**

½ tablespoon **GROUND BLACK PEPPER**

Italian Seasoning

Yield: About ⅔ cup

3 tablespoons **DRIED PARSLEY**

3 tablespoons **DRIED BASIL**

2 tablespoons **DRIED OREGANO**

2 teaspoons **DRIED MARJORAM**

1 tablespoon **GARLIC POWDER**

1 teaspoon **DRIED ROSEMARY**

1 teaspoon **DRIED THYME**

1 teaspoon **ONION POWDER**

½ teaspoons **DRIED RED CHILE PEPPER FLAKES**

¼ teaspoons **GROUND BLACK PEPPER**

Italian Bread Dip Seasoning

Yield: About ⅓ cup

1 tablespoon **DRIED OREGANO**

1 tablespoon **DRIED MINCED ONION**

1 tablespoon **DRIED BASIL**

1 tablespoon **DRIED PARSLEY**

1 tablespoon **GARLIC POWDER**

½ tablespoon **DRIED MINCED GARLIC**

2 teaspoon **DRIED ROSEMARY**

2 teaspoon **DRIED RED CHILE PEPPER FLAKES**

1 teaspoon **DRIED THYME**

½ teaspoon **GROUND BLACK PEPPER**

Instructions:

1. Put the larger spices (rosemary, dehydrated garlic, red pepper, onion) in a Ziploc bag and roll over it with a rolling pin. A couple of times should do it, you don't want to pulverize them into a powder.
2. Mix crushed spices with the rest of the ingredients and mix well.

To use: Pour a thin layer of olive oil in a flat dish and drizzle some balsamic vinegar on top, then sprinkle a layer of the spices over the top.

Mexicali Seasoning

Yield: About ½ cup

2 tablespoons **DRIED CILANTRO**

2 tablespoons **CHILI POWDER**

1 tablespoon **GROUND CUMIN**

2 teaspoons **GROUND CHIPOTLE PEPPER**

2 teaspoons **COARSE SEA SALT**

2 teaspoons **PAPRIKA**

1 ½ teaspoons **DRIED OREGANO**

1 teaspoon **GARLIC POWDER**

1 teaspoon **ONION POWDER**

Onion and Garlic Seasoning Mix

Yield: Between ¾ and 1 cup

¼ cup **GARLIC POWDER**

¼ cup **ONION POWDER**

¼ cup **DRIED PARSLEY**

1 tablespoon **FINE SALT**

½ tablespoons **GROUND BLACK PEPPER**

Parmesan Pizza Seasoning

Yield: Between ½ and ⅔ cup

½ cup **GRATED PARMESAN CHEESE**

1 teaspoon **DRIED BASIL**

1 teaspoon **DRIED OREGANO**

1 teaspoon **DRIED RED CHILE PEPPER FLAKES**

½ teaspoons **GARLIC POWDER**

½ teaspoons **FINE SALT**

*Sprinkle on hot pizza before serving & store extra seasoning mix in the refrigerator.

Poultry Seasoning

Yield: About ⅓ cup

2 tablespoons **GROUND SAGE**

1 tablespoon **GROUND THYME**

1 tablespoon **GROUND MARJORAM**

2 ½ teaspoons **GROUND ROSEMARY**

1 ½ teaspoons **GROUND NUTMEG**

1 ½ teaspoons **CRACKED BLACK PEPPER**

Rotisserie Seasoning

Yield: About 1 cup

3 tablespoons **FLAKY SALT**

2 tablespoons **PAPRIKA** (regular or smoked or a mix of both)

2 tablespoons **ONION POWDER**

2 tablespoons **GARLIC POWDER**

2 tablespoons **ITALIAN SEASONING**

2 tablespoons **BROWN SUGAR**

1 tablespoon **DRIED THYME**

1 tablespoon **DRIED MUSTARD POWDER**

1 tablespoon **GROUND CAYENNE PEPPER**

1 tablespoon **GROUND BLACK PEPPER**

Spicy Fish Seasoning

Yield: About ⅔ cup

2 tablespoons **GARLIC POWDER**

2 tablespoons **FINE SALT**

2 tablespoons **PAPRIKA**

1 tablespoon **ONION POWDER**

1 tablespoon **GROUND BLACK PEPPER**

1 tablespoon **DRIED OREGANO**

1 tablespoon **DRIED THYME**

1 ½ teaspoon **GROUND CAYENNE PEPPER** (or to taste)

Southwest Seasoning

Yield: About ¼ cup

1 tablespoon **GARLIC POWDER**

1 tablespoon **CHILI POWDER**

1 tablespoon **ONION POWDER**

1 tablespoon **SMOKED PAPRIKA**

2 teaspoons **GROUND CUMIN**

½ teaspoon **GROUND CHIPOTLE CHILE PEPPER**

Sweet Potato Seasoning

Yield: About ¼ cup

2 tablespoons **FINE SALT**

1 tablespoon **GROUND BLACK PEPPER**

2 teaspoons **GROUND CINNAMON**

1 teaspoon **GROUND CAYENNE PEPPER**

Tex-Mex Seasoning

Yield: About ¼ cup

1 tablespoon **CHILI POWDER**

2 teaspoons **PAPRIKA**

2 teaspoons **GROUND CUMIN**

1 teaspoon **GARLIC POWDER**

1 teaspoon **ONION POWDER**

½ teaspoon **DRIED RED CHILE PEPPER FLAKES**

½ teaspoon **DRIED OREGANO**

½ teaspoon **GROUND BLACK PEPPER**

1 pinch **GROUND CINNAMON**

1 pinch **GROUND CLOVES**

1 tablespoon **FLAKY SEA SALT** (optional)

Thai Seasoning

Yield: About ¼ cup

2 tablespoons **UNSWEETENED DRIED SHREDDED COCONUT**

1 ½ tablespoons **PAPRIKA**

1 tablespoon **WHOLE BLACK PEPPERCORNS** (reduce for less heat)

2 teaspoon **GROUND TURMERIC**

1 teaspoon **GROUND CORIANDER**

1 teaspoon **DRY MUSTARD POWDER**

1 teaspoon **GROUND CUMIN**

1 teaspoon **GROUND GINGER**

½ teaspoon **GROUND CAYENNE** or **SERRANO POWDER** (optional)

Instructions:

1. Grind coconut and peppercorns until coconut is mostly a powder.
2. Add the rest of the ingredients and pulse until everything is well blended.

<u>**Vegetable Seasoning**</u>

Yield: Between ⅓ and ½ cup

2 tablespoons **DRIED MINCED ONION**

2 tablespoons **ONION POWDER**

2 tablespoons **GARLIC POWDER**

2 teaspoons **GARLIC SALT**

1 teaspoon **GROUND BLACK PEPPER**

<u>**Wasabi Seaweed Seasoning**</u>

Yield: About 1 cup

2-3 full sheets **ROASTED NORI** (dried seaweed sheets)

½ cup **WASABI PEAS**

1 teaspoon **COARSE SEA SALT**

<u>Instructions:</u>

1. Break up seaweed sheets, so they fit in a spice grinder or food processor. Pulse a few times until it is broken down into small pieces.
2. Add wasabi peas and salt and pulse until everything mostly ground and well blended.
3. Use a fork to pick out any large bits of unground wasabi peas.

Seasoned
Salts

Cajun Salt

Yield: About ¾ cup

½ tablespoon **GROUND BLACK PEPPER**

½ tablespoon **CHILI POWDER**

2 teaspoons **GROUND CAYENNE PEPPER**

½ teaspoon **CUMIN SEEDS**

½ teaspoon **GROUND BAY LEAF**

½ teaspoon **DRIED BASIL**

½ teaspoon **DRIED THYME**

½ tablespoon **ONION POWDER**

½ tablespoon **GARLIC POWDER**

½ teaspoon **PAPRIKA**

½ teaspoon **DRIED OREGANO**

½ cup **COARSE SEA SALT**

Instructions:

1. Add all the seasoning, except salt, in a blender.
2. Cover and blend to a fine consistency.
3. Add blended spices and salt to a bowl and stir until you achieve a uniform color.

Chile-Lime Salt

Yield: About ¼ cup

2 tablespoons **FLAKY SALT**

1 teaspoon **GROUND ANCHO CHILE POWDER**

2 **LIMES**, zested

Instructions:

1. Preheat oven to 350°F. Toss salt and chili powder on a baking sheet. Finely zest 2 limes over.
2. Bake, occasionally stirring, until lime zest is dry, about 5 minutes. Let cool.

Spicy Chile-Lime Salt

Yield: About ¼ cup

2 tablespoons **FLAKY SALT**

1 teaspoon **GROUND CAYENNE PEPPER**

2 **LIMES**, zested

Instructions:

1. Preheat oven to 350°F. Toss salt and chili powder on a baking sheet. Finely zest 2 limes over.
2. Bake, occasionally stirring, until lime zest is dry, about 5 minutes. Let cool.

Chinese Five-Spice Salt

Yield: A little less than ½ cup

2 tablespoons **GROUND ANISE**

1 tablespoon **GROUND BLACK PEPPER**

1 tablespoon **GROUND FENNEL**

1 tablespoon **GROUND CINNAMON**

1 tablespoon **GROUND CLOVES**

1 tablespoon **COARSE SEA SALT**

Chipotle-Lime Salt

Yield: About ¼ cup

2 tablespoons **FLAKY SALT**

1 teaspoon **GROUND CHIPOTLE CHILE PEPPER**

2 **LIMES**, zested

Instructions:

1. Preheat oven to 350°F. Toss salt and chili powder on a baking sheet. Finely zest 2 limes over.
2. Bake, occasionally stirring, until lime zest is dry, about 5 minutes. Let cool.

Citrus & Herb Salt

Yield: Just over 1 cup

¾ cup **COARSE SEA SALT**

2 tablespoons **DRIED LEMON ZEST**

4 teaspoons **DRIED ROSEMARY**

3 teaspoons **DRIED THYME**

3 teaspoons **DRIED OREGANO**

½ teaspoon **SUGAR**

½ teaspoon **PAPRIKA**

½ teaspoon **DRIED RED CHILE PEPPER FLAKES**

Coffee-Paprika Salt

Yield: About ¼ cup

2 tablespoons **FLAKY SALT**

1 tablespoon **FRESHLY GROUND COFFEE**

1 tablespoon **HOT SMOKED PAPRIKA**

Herbes de Provence Salt

Yield: About ⅔ cup

½ cup **COARSE SEA SALT**

2 teaspoons **CULINARY LAVENDER**

½ teaspoon **FRESH THYME**

½ teaspoon **FRESH ROSEMARY**

½ teaspoon **FRESH OREGANO**

½ teaspoon **FRESH SAGE**

½ teaspoon **DRIED SAVORY**

½ teaspoon **DRIED MARJORAM**

Instructions:

1. Loosely chop all of the fresh herbs and place them in a spice grinder or food processor. Pulse a few times or until fine.
2. Add the dried herbs, lavender, and ¼ cup salt—pulse 2 to 3 more times.
3. Empty into a mixing bowl and stir in the remaining salt—place in a glass container and store in a cool, dry place.

*Although this blend uses fresh herbs, it will keep in the cupboard for several weeks — but I always store mine in the fridge.

Sage, Rosemary, and Garlic Salt (easy & fast)

Yield: About ½ cup

¼ cup **COARSE SEA SALT**

2 tablespoons **DRIED SAGE**

2 tablespoons **DRIED ROSEMARY**

1 tablespoon **DRIED MINCED GARLIC**

Instructions:

1. Place all ingredients in a small food processor and pulse until fine.

Sage, Rosemary, and Garlic Salt (difficult & long)

Yield: About ⅔ cup

½ cup **FRESH SAGE LEAVES**

½ cup **FRESH ROSEMARY LEAVES**

3-5 **GARLIC CLOVES**, peeled

¼ cup **COARSE SEA SALT**

Instructions:

1. Remove leaves from the woodier stems and place them in a small food processor and pulse until fine.
2. Add garlic and pulse until the garlic is minced
3. Add the salt and pulse until everything is very fine and thoroughly combined.
4. Spread the mixture in a thin layer on a small baking sheet and place it in an oven on the lowest setting possible and leave the door open 4-6 inches for 1-3 hours. Check often and use a spatula to stir the mixture.
5. The drying process is done when the mixture is noticeably lighter colored, and you feel no moisture when you take a pinch of it between your fingers. Use a fork or spatula to break up any larger clumps. Let cool completely.

Sichuan Salt

Yield: About ½ cup

2 ½ tablespoons **SICHUAN PEPPERCORNS**

2 ½ tablespoons **CUMIN SEEDS**

2 ½ tablespoons **COARSE SEA SALT**

Instructions:

1. In a small skillet over medium heat, add all the ingredients and heat, often stirring, until spices are toasted and very fragrant, about 3 minutes.
2. Transfer to a bowl; let cool.
3. Finely grind the mixture in a spice mill or in a mortar with a pestle.

*Sichuan peppercorns are available at some specialty foods stores and at Asian markets.

Sichuan-Sesame Salt

Yield: About ¼ cup

2 tablespoons **FLAKY SALT**

1 tablespoon **SESAME SEEDS**

1 tablespoon **SICHUAN PEPPERCORNS**

1 teaspoon **DRIED RED CHILE PEPPER FLAKES**

<u>Instructions:</u>

1. Preheat oven to 350°F. Coarsely grind peppercorns and red pepper flakes. Toss on a rimmed baking sheet with salt and sesame seeds.
2. Bake, occasionally stirring, until fragrant, about 5 minutes. Let cool.

Sriracha Salt

Yield: About 1 cup

1 cup **COARSE SEA SALT**

1 to 2 tablespoons **SRIRACHA SAUCE**

Instructions:

1. Stir the Sriracha and the salt together thoroughly. Spread it out into a thin layer on a dry baking sheet and set in the sun for 1 to 2 days, dry it in a dehydrator, or in an oven set at 100°F overnight until dry.
2. When completely dry, break up any clumps with your fingers or a spoon and transfer it to a container with a tight-fitting lid.

Tabasco (Green or Red) Salt

Yield: About 1 cup

1 cup **COARSE SEA SALT**

1 - 2 tablespoons (green or red) **TABASCO SAUCE**

Instructions:

1. Stir the tabasco and the salt together thoroughly. Spread it out into a thin layer on a dry baking sheet and set in the sun for 1 to 2 days, dry it in a dehydrator, or in an oven set at 100°F overnight until dry.
2. When completely dry, break up any clumps with your fingers or a spoon and transfer it to a container with a tight-fitting lid.

Toasted Seasoning Salt

Yield: About ¾ cup

¼ cup **COARSE SEA SALT**

¼ cup **COARSELY GROUND BLACK PEPPER**

¼ cup **GARLIC POWDER**

Instructions:

1. In a large dry skillet, cook salt over medium-low heat for 5 minutes, stirring constantly. Don't let it burn-just toasted. Remove and cool completely.
2. In a bowl, sift salt, pepper, and garlic powder until well blended. Store in an airtight container for up to 3 months.

<u>Toasty Smoky Spicy Seasoning Salt</u>

Yield: About ¾ cup

¼ cup **COARSE SEA SALT**

¼ cup **COARSELY GROUND BLACK PEPPER**

¼ cup **GARLIC POWDER**

1 tablespoon **GROUND CHIPOTLE CHILE PEPPER**

<u>Instructions:</u>

1. In a large dry skillet, cook salt over medium-low heat for 5 minutes, stirring constantly. Don't let it burn-just toasted. Remove and cool completely.
2. In a bowl, sift salt, pepper, garlic powder, and chipotle until well blended. Store in an airtight container for up to 3 months.

Conversion
Charts

Dry Measurements by Weight (approximate):

Recipe Says	Also equals	Ounces	Grams
nip	1/64 tsp		
shake	1/32 tsp		
pinch	1/16 tsp	.01 oz	.25 g
dash	⅛ tsp	.02 oz	.5 g
¼ tsp	tad	.04 oz	1 g
½ tsp		.08 oz	2 g
¾ tsp		.125 oz	3 g
1 tsp		.17 oz	4 g
1 ½ tsp	½ tbsp	.25 oz	9 g
1 tbsp	3 tsp	.5 oz	14 g
2 tbsp	6 tsp	1 oz	28 g
¼ cup	4 tbsp	2 oz	56 g
⅓ cup	5 tbsp + 1 tsp	2.66 oz	75 g
½ cup	8 tbsp	4 oz	113 g
⅔ cup	10 tbsp + 2 tsp	5.33 oz	151 g
¾ cup	12 tbsp	6 oz	170 g
1 cup	16 tbsp	8 oz	225 g
2 cups	32 tbsp	16 oz	454 g
4 cups	64 tbsp	32 oz	907 g

Salt Substitutions

Equal Salt Substitutions

Recipe Says	Appropriate Substitute
Table Salt	Fine Sea Salt, Fine Pink Salt, Canning & Pickling Salt
Kosher Salt	Coarse Sea Salt, Coarse Pink Salt, Fine Sea Salt, Canning/Pickling Salt
Coarse Sea Salt	Coarse Pink Salt, Kosher Salt
Fine Sea Salt	Natural Sea Salt, Fine Pink Salt, Table Salt, Canning/Pickling Salt
Coarse Pink Salt	Coarse Sea Salt, Kosher Salt
Fine Pink Salt	Fine Sea Salt, Natural Sea Salt
Natural Sea Salt	Fine Sea Salt, Fine Pink Salt, Table Salt, Canning/Pickling Salt
Canning/Pickling Salt	Natural Sea Salt, Fine Sea Salt, Kosher Salt

Unequal Salt Substitutions

Coarse Sea Salt	Kosher Salt	Table Salt	Fine Sea Salt	Flaky Salt
¼ tsp	¼ tsp	¼ tsp	¼ tsp	½ tsp
1 tsp	1 ¼ tsp	1 tsp	1 tsp	2 tsp
1 tbsp	1 tbsp + 1 tsp	1 tbsp	1 tbsp	2 tbsp
¼ cup	¼ cup + 1 ¼ tsp	3 ½ tbsp	3 ½ tbsp	½ cup
⅓ cup	⅓ cup + ½ tbsp	¼ cup + 2 ½ tsp	¼ cup + 2 ½ tsp	⅔ cup
½ cup	½ cup + 2 ½ tsp	⅓ cup +2 tbsp	⅓ cup + 2 tbsp	1 cup
⅔ cup	⅔ cup + 1 tbsp	½ cup + 1 ½ tbsp	½ cup + 1 ½ tbsp	1 ⅓ cups
¾ cup	¾ cup + 1 tbsp	⅔ cup + ½ tsp	⅔ cup + ½ tsp	1 ½ cups
1 cup	1 cup + 1 ½ tbsp	¾ cup + 2 ½ tbsp	¾ cup + 2 ½ tbsp	2 cups

Fresh, Whole, Dried, Granulated, Ground, and Powdered Herb Substitutions

FRESH HERBS are just that, fresh and will require prepping.

DRIED HERBS have a flaky texture and the pieces are discernable from each other.

GRANULATED HERBS have a sand grain appearance.

GROUND HERBS and **POWDERS** have a powdery texture.

WHOLE SPICES will be dry like seeds, nuts, and cinnamon sticks; they will usually require at a minimum crushing or grinding but sometimes toasting too.

Fresh, Dried, & Ground Herb Substitutions

Fresh to dried - 3 to 1	Dried to fresh - 1 to 3
Fresh to ground - 4 to 1	Ground to fresh - 1 to 4
Recipe calls for	**Substitute**
1 teaspoon dried herb	3 teaspoons fresh herb
1 teaspoon ground herb	4 teaspoons fresh herb
3 teaspoons fresh herb	1 teaspoon dried herb
4 teaspoons fresh herb	1 teaspoon ground herb

Whole Spice Equivalents & Substitutions

Spice	Amount Whole	Equals Ground
Allspice berries	1 tsp allspice berries	¾ tsp
Anise seeds	1 tsp	¾ tsp
Cardamom pods	20 pods = 2 tsp pods dehusked = 1 tsp seeds	¾ tsp
Caraway seeds	1 tsp	¾ tsp
Celery seeds	1 tsp	¾ tsp
Cinnamon stick	1 (3-inch) piece	1 tsp
Cloves	1 tsp	¾ tsp
Coriander seeds	1 tsp	¾ tsp
Cumin seeds	1 tsp	¾ tsp
Dill seeds	1 tsp	¾ tsp
Fennel seeds	1 tsp	¾ tsp
Juniper berries	1 tsp	¾ tsp
Mustard seeds	1 tsp	¾ tsp
Nutmeg	½ nutmeg	1 tsp
Peppercorns	1 tsp	¾ tsp

Rhizomes & Alliums Equivalents & Substitutions (Bulbs & Roots)

Onion

Size	Fresh Chopped	Fresh Minced	Dried Flakes	Dried Minced	Granulated	Powder
Small	⅓ cup	2 ½ t	1 tbsp	½ tsp	1 tsp	1 tsp
Medium	½ cup	¼ cup	3 tbsp	1 ½ tsp	1 tbsp	1 tbsp
Large	1 ½ cup	¾ cup	4 ½ tbsp	2 ¼ tsp	1 ½ tbsp	1 ½ tbsp

Garlic

Clove Size	Fresh Minced	Jarred Minced	Dried Minced	Granulated	Powder
1 small	½ tsp	½ tsp	¼ tsp	⅛ tsp	⅛ tsp
1 medium	1 tsp	1 tsp	½ tsp	¼ tsp	¼ tsp
1 large	1 ½ tsp	1 ½ tsp	¾ tsp	½ tsp	½ tsp
1 extra large	2 tsp	2 tsp	1 tsp	¾ tsp	¾ tsp

Ginger & Turmeric

Ginger Length	Fresh Chopped	Fresh Minced	Powder
1 (3-inch) piece	2 tbsp	1 tbsp	¼- ½ tsp

Turmeric Length	Fresh Chopped	Fresh Minced	Powder
1 (1-inch) piece	2 tbsp	1 tbsp	1 tsp

Recipe Index

About the Author

USA Today Bestselling Author, Emmy Gatrell loves food and has written several cookbooks for her newsletter subscribers; she finally got off her butt and started publishing them for everyone to enjoy. She also writes in multiple fiction genres, including epic fantasy, urban fantasy, paranormal romance, dystopian, speculative fiction, and supernatural horror ranging from young adult through four-flame +18.

Emmy is also a Stay-At-Homeschool-Mom to two young men, nine dogs, and a husband. She grew up in Metro-Detroit and graduated with a Theatre/Speech Communications degree from Siena Heights University in Adrian, Michigan, before moving to Georgia. A decade later, her family realized it was still too cold and now call Costa Rica home. There it's always summer—and the seasons are kind of dry, rainy, and deluge.

If you're interested in learning more about Emmy's novels or cookbooks, check out her website http://emmygatrell.com/!

<u>Follow Emmy on Social Media:</u>

Facebook: Author Emmy Gatrell

Instagram: @emgatrell

Twitter: @emmyeg

Bookbub: Emmy Gatrell

Goodreads: Emmy Gatrell

Other Books By the Author

Cookbooks

No Frills Cookbook Collection:
Volume One: Be Basic - Spice Cabinet Staples
Volume Two: Around the World in 80 Ways - Exotic Spice Blends
Volume Three: Rub it Down - BBQ & Dry Rub Recipes
Volume Four: Marinades For the Rest of Us – Easy & Delicious Marinades
Volume Five: Around the World in 80 Marinades – Exotic Marinades

Epic YA/NA Fantasy

The Daearen Realms Series:
Book One: Meanmna
Book Two: Bienn-Theine
Book Three: Eitlean

Adult Urban Fantasy/Paranormal Romance

The Lupinski Clan Series:
Book One: Fate is a Mated Bitch
Book Two: Cords of Fate
Book Three: Forgiving Fate
Book Four: Full Moon's Fate
Book Five: Fateful Wish

Want a printable copy of the charts to keep handy?

Sign-up for Emmy's Newsletter and get a set for FREE!

https://www.subscribepage.com/nofrillscookbook

Sweet, Saucy, Spicy Speculative Fiction & Fantasy

emmy gatrell